DEVELOPING YOUR-SELF

Year of First Printing, 2017

ISBN: 9781365934858

115 Douglas Road, Owerri.

Owerri, Imo State, 460001

E-mail: jmsokere@gmail.com

www.inspireforgreatness.com

DEDICATION

To all those who would think deep, discover their purpose, believing themselves and willing to work hard to purse a cause that would impact humanity and society; I dedicate this book to.

ACKNOWLEDGEMENT

I acknowledge the inputs of all those who supported the publication of my previous works. Your encouragement energized me to write this book: Developing Your-Self.

Mrs. Adelyn Nkechi Okere (my lovely wife) gave me wonderful assistance in producing this work. To her and indeed my family, I remain ever grateful. To Odinakachukwu Onwuatuogu-my online assistant, I thank you.

Let me also acknowledge the inputs made by inspirational authors, speakers and writers, whose works I have come across. These people include Napoleon Hill, John C. Maxwell, Dr. Ben Carson, Bill Newman, John Mason, Rev. Dr. Chris E. Kwakpovwe, Ebele Toni, Norman Vincent Peale, etc. I owe them greatly for spurring me to write this book.

Finally, I am grateful to Nnamdi Ogwazu, a Blogger, Public Affairs Commentator, Journalist, Social Entrepreneur, Public Speaker and a great mind who not only accepted to foreword this book but contributed immensely to its making.

James Ngozi Okere

FOREWORD

Developing Your-Self is a life changing and inspirational book geared towards helping one realize himself. The book will enable somebody recognize his potentials and work towards developing same accordingly.
The issues discussed in the book is to challenge one to confront and attack those inhibitive and prohibitive forces holding you back from attaining your divine purpose in life. The thoughts shared in this book will no doubt go a long way towards developing the readers, igniting your innate abilities to break through barriers, reach new heights and live true to your dreams, thus developing positive impacts towards advancing humanity and society.

The author, James Okere who is a public speaker, an inspirational blogger and author strongly believes in the power of self development and creative thinking. In this book the author has challenge us to strive to develop one's potentials, to enable you achieve great accomplishments capable of affecting your generations. He opined and advice strongly that one must apply his mind and direct it towards conceiving productive ideas that would improve one's personality and societal advancement; this is a challenge to all who would want to develop himself/herself.

In Chapter One, the author presents clearly his idea of what developing oneself stood for; anchored on faith in God and the discovery of life core issues leading to accomplishments recognized by the society. -

In Chapter Two, Okere reveals the importance of vision in achieving self development. While in Chapter Three and Four, the author brought out the powers associated with reading and talents development respectively towards life accomplishments.

In Chapter Five, the author encouraged readers not to be discouraged but to look beyond their challenges as the process of self developing involves trials and difficulties.

In Chapter Six, Okere discusses on the success associated in self development, while in Chapter Seven the author highlighted persons who faced their challenges squirrelly and developed themselves in spite of difficulties.

In Chapter Eight, the author reveals thoughts of men that propel successes in human beings. Finally, in Chapter Nine, the author brought out those salient values that inspire one and spring up life consciousness into great men and women.

The author who is an inspirational writer, political scientist, and public speaker and promising researcher brings to bare, his intellectual prowess in presenting a synoptic account of life experiences of some people, who through dint of self discovery, hard work, dogged determination and manifest obstacles rose to prominence and stardom.

By focusing on their success stories, James Okere re-emphasizes that the power or ability to make, develop, and achieve a desired result is of the mind. He further cautions that things do not happen, and you should not just dream because you can dream dreams. Dream because of the difference you would want to make.

The author admits that man or environment might become a stumbling block and a hindrance to your vision. But your faith in God and the confidence you have in yourself will help you weather the storm. Okere further opines that the reader is endowed with special qualities that should be developed with absolute faith in God.

In addition, the author in his epilogue challenged all to develop strong positive core values which develop one towards advancing in any society for positive growth.

I commend James Okere for this life changing and inspirational treatise on developing yourself. This book will be very useful for all.

Awake, be courageous and develop yourself.

NNAMDI OGWAZU,
Blogger, Public Affairs Commentator, Journalist, Social Entrepreneur and Public Speaker.

PREFACE

Developing Your-Self is a life changing and inspirational book written to help one build values that would further galvanize the reader. The contents of the book would galvanize one towards achieving success attested to by the society. The book is designed to assist one remain focused and painstaking in any planned programme or destiny fulfillment.

In addition, the book Developing Your-Self further opined that in individual boldness, self-will, dogged determination, perseverance and organized planning lies the values of self development. Self development leads to creative thinking towards achieving greatness and success.

Added to the book are illustrations on few persons who, in spite of all challenges, defined their goals and created values to become successful through achieving tremendous accomplishments. Today, humanity and society attest to contributions of these people.

The few personalities mentioned in this book are to illustrate that the mind that is developed, focused and undaunted can rise up to greater accomplishments in spite of hiccups.

James Ngozi Okere.

CHAPTER ONE

CORE ISSUES IN DEVELOPING YOUR SELF

The process of developing oneself is built around obstacles, unfriendly environment, trials, failures and errors. But in individual boldness, self-will, dogged determination, perseverance and organized planning lies the values of self development. Self development leads to creative thinking towards achieving greatness and success.

It is a known fact that people complain of the adverse conditions of their environment; let it be known that adverse conditions would continue so long that man lives on this planet earth. What one requires is the boldness to confront adverse situations towards greater accomplishments.
All over the world, it is evident that historically, no nation or human race has ever witnessed continuous friendly environment without setbacks. But suffice it to say that the few nations or persons that succeeded are those who made self-discoveries, marrying same with determination, in spite of the prevalent circumstances of their time; to attain greatness.

Empires were achieved by men who developed themselves and believed in their cause, and pursued same with great determination. Therefore, the key to develop oneself lies in the thought or mind process rooted in a designed road map of an individual. The essence of self development is to become successful in any chosen field in line with one's destiny; including technological advancement, politics, academics, sports, business, writing, skilled and unskilled professions, religious activities etc attested to by the people, thus impacting positively on human development.

Self development can be achieved with or without formal education, but it requires individual concerted and self- development efforts in the individual's chosen profession, thus creating value in the society.

Therefore, the core issues in self development include:

PRAYER

Napoleon Hill and C. Harold Keown in their book, "Succeed and Grow Rich Through Persuasion" on prayer recorded:

> ***"Express a prayer of gratitude at least twice daily, just before retiring at night and just after rising in the morning, for the blessings you now possess as well as for the things you expect to attain in the future".***

From the above, we can do nothing except one commits his actions or plans into God's hand for his guidance.

Prayer to God on our stated goals grants us the faith, trust and confidence in God which gives us the grace for accomplishment. No achievement, no matter how big or small, can be made without the blessings of God to which we have a right through prayer.

Prayer liberates one from spiritual bondage thereby granting one the peace of mind to work assiduously towards developing oneself. A strong relationship with God through prayer gives one assurance and courage to pursue a course of action, and to sustain us even when we fail the first or second time.
In all attributes of self development lies divine connection which provides one with unshaken faith, purpose and positive mental attitude to destroy the strongholds of the enemy, including self-defeatism.

CREATING ENERGY

No successful venture is ever achieved without strong personal energy. For one to develop and succeed, one must decide to be propelled by desire and enthusiasm. Visualizing the gains of the individual goal is a sure way of constantly putting our energy into force, thus developing the magic wand to stir one's blood to accomplishments.
If not for creation of energy, history would not have recorded Thomas Carlyle as the author of the French Revolution book. Carlyle after working for two years, produced the manuscript of his book, sent same to his friend John Staut Mill for

proof-reading. In the process, Mill lost the manuscript, but Carlyle after feeling bad about this development, later consoled himself, and went back to work and finally produced his book on the French Revolution.

REMAIN FOCUS

The mind that is focused has the pedigree for success. Concentrating on your stated task will provide the magic wand for upliftment. Consistent focus leads to pressing on which has solved the problems of the human race.

Thomas Edison failed several times in his quest to provide man with electric bulb. But in spite of Edison's predicaments he remained focused and eventually achieved his target, thereby adding value to human development.

GENERATING IDEAS

This is the management of ideas pursued in line with one's planned goals for attainment of greater accomplishment. You must dream on your task as to change the course of history. Your memory motivation must be constantly sustained so as to visualize the victory ahead which is achieved gradually.

Mr. Frank Nneji, a Zoology graduate, challenged his thought process, and moved into the transport business in Nigeria. He introduced style and innovative transportation which created strong value for travelers with his "A.B.C. Transport". Today, by his power of thinking, he has aided in empowering the society.

SENSE OF CREATIVITY

Many great men have used their sense of personal initiatives and discipline to develop and turn around unfriendly circumstances into positive values. To succeed, these people developed high level of determination to work, employing the principle of going the extra mile.

Personal initiative and discipline will motivate one to think inwardly and utilize the powers lying in him to discover resources and harness same for greater successes in an endeavour.

HARD WORK

Hard work is the key to greater accomplishments in life pursuits hence the saying, striving for success without hard work is like trying to harvest where you did not sow. When a goal or target is being pursued, one must develop the will power to work as to succeed.

In self development, we should note that initial failures, predicaments or disappointments should not deter one, but trust in God, continuous adjustments or work will propel one into achieving success in life. One who employs extra-mile and dependent principles in developing himself/ herself is bound to succeed, thereby contributing towards societal development.

In self development, you demonstrate yourself to the world. Nothing succeeds than being oneself. You should decide to locate your God-given talents in order to add value to the society. Self- manifestation achieves victory in inches in the short run, and in miles in the long run. Mother Tereser and Mahatma Gandhi manifested their simple life style with which they influenced society.
You might develop your talents to defend the downtrodden as Chief Gani Fawehinmi (a Nigerian) is noted for. If you have the talent to write as to influence individuals and societies you must develop same as Benjamin Disreali (former British Prime-Minister) and Benjamin Franklyn (American Man of Letters) are noted for.

Florence Nightingale, born into a wealthy family in London, delved into the nursing profession contrary to the expectations of her wealthy parents who never supported her nursing profession. But her experience as a nurse and interactions with sick persons led her to publish notes on how hospitals should be operated. Florence's determination influenced the nature and structure of today's hospital management.

Developing oneself towards success and greatness entails using your occupation and talents vide hard work, determination and enthusiasm to reach greater height in your identified field in spite of disabilities or unfriendly environment. The essence of greatness is to influence the society positively as to advance the cause of human development.

In self development, success achieved should genuinely be attested to by the people. It has nothing to do with mere flowing in money, but rather flowing in wealth as a result of conscientious efforts attested to by the society, thereby creating positive value on the psyche of the people.

In working towards self development, one must define his or her goals; cultivate energy, patience and hard work to rise in one's endeavour.
The roadmap to achieving success through self development is a challenging one, that any person desirous must power himself into action and not mere wish.
In addition, self development involves career development and remodeling imbued with zeal and going the extra mile. Chief Emmanuel C. Adiele (a former Minister of Communication), Chartered Accountant and a key player in Nigeria financial sector started work as a clerk.

Age is also not a barrier towards attaining self development. Yours could come up early or later in life depending on the plans of God. Your will power for self-discovery, hard work, determination and an eye to see genuine opportunity are factors towards achieving success.

Furthermore, in the pursuit of self development towards life accomplishments, the inner will must be kept in constant positive mental attitude and purpose- driven, thereby manifesting clear picture of the things to accomplish in life. Self-doubts should be discarded, while your talents must be identified and developed through hard work, diligence and positive faith in God.
Also, self development connotes developing strong idea, desire, faith, imagination, persistence and the power of the mastermind. The mind desirous of greatness, therefore, must develop good public image which includes being empathic, friendly, respecting the opinion of others and service to humanity.

CHAPTER TWO

ACTIVATE YOUR VISION

"Intensify your dreams and you will reach them faster than you would have ever imagined" (Daniel Ally, founder of Ally Way International).The creator of the universe in the Holy Book of Habakkuk instructed us to write down our vision. The creator knowing the importance of vision further stated in the book of Proverbs that my people perish for lack of vision.

Individuals are developed through vision they champion. Organizations are coordinated effectively through vision of people. The same goes to the society; which develops because men sat down, gave thought and developed a vision to follow.

As we are creators of God, we are naturally endowed with creative powers to develop vision of what we would want to be or accomplish in life as to impact society. The first issue for consideration towards vision development is to align one's self with the talents, abilities and potentials endowed in one by the Creator. The drive to align our vision with our talents is to enable have a long lasting dream that would out live one after death.

Many who have developed their vision even though dead are still made a reference point; signifying that they developed themselves. People are still living under the goodwill of Dr. Myles Munroe, Zig Ziglar, Charles Dickens, Fanny Hurst, Barr. Gani Fawhenmi, Dr. Nelson Mandela etc, though these men were dead, their legacies still speaks for them. Their goodwill is still feeding many today.

In developing our vision, we should identify where one is, what one has done and have total review of one's life as to gather strength towards advancing one's vision. In addition, what a person wants to achieve in line with one's gifts also energize one's vision.

When a vision has been identified, it would be powered or put into action, without action, a vision becomes a mere dream. Preston Vander ven (an online marketing expert) says ***"A dream with no action is just a wish"***. In powering a vision, one should become creative and demonstrate commitment towards his dream project. In addition, one must develop courage and persistence, and be proactive. Courage and perseverance will give one the energy for sustainability.

Through your developed dream, you are to show yourself to the world. Nothing succeeds than one working to see his dream come through. You must decide to power your dream through locating your God-given talents in order to add value to the society. Pursuits of one's dream leads to achieving victory in inches in the short run, and in miles in the long run. If you have the dream to manifest humility of life with which to influence the society as Mahatma Gandhi did to influence Indians, continue with such dream.

You might have a dream to defend the downtrodden as Chief Gani Fawehinmi (a Nigerian Lawyer) is noted for. You might have the dream to write as to influence individuals and societies; to achieve such dream you must push the idea forward as Benjamin Franklyn (American Man of Letters) was noted for. In spite of opposition he faced even from his brother, towards developing his writing talents, Benjamin continued and ended up achieving his dream of being a renowned author in the world.

To inspire and bring out the best in people, Eugene Lang started a foundation called **"I have a Dream".** Eugene Lang was an American and a successful entrepreneur. He was also Success Magazine **"Successful Man''** of the Year in 1986. He is a strong believer that encouragement brings the best in man.

Lang used the foundation- **"I have a Dream"**, he started to inspire hope amongst the citizens by going into class rooms to speak to Americans to inculcate positive values. Because of the tremendous impact of his programme, other American entrepreneurs copied his model. His idea further inspired the United States Congress, that introduced same for a nationwide education programme called **"GEAR UP",** which started in 1998 to inspire American students to think what to become in future; a demonstration of the power of vision.

In demonstrating his dream project, Eugene Lang applied the principle of staying power; which sustained him tremendously. Imagine he left his idea when he faced initial challenges occasioned by people's own thinking. The result today would have been that history would not have recorded a positive place for him in United States of America.

The message is that our ideas once generated are achievable if we believe in God and believe in ourselves and apply the doing concepts of determination, powering

oneself into action, admit that greatness is in your hand, keep trying and develop yourself accordingly.

CHAPTER THREE

POWER OF READING

The power of reading is a great virtue in human development. Reading occupies an important position in self development. Reading will build in any person with new knowledge, information and skills needed to contribute towards society which aid in sustainable development.

Reading will give anybody that embraces it the motivation and skills to contribute towards transforming their societies into safe, secure and productive environments.

Therefore, in the process of self development, reading will inspire one and another to engage each other on how to make contributions towards promoting sustainable values including ending poverty in the society. Their engaging one and another would create awareness and build peace in the land to work on projects that would build human capacity development and maintenance of peace. Peace promotes democracy which works towards sustaining positive change in the society including self development for self discovery towards societal development.

Dr. Ben Carson a world known Neurologist stated "There is just no limit to what people can accomplish when they develop their minds and use book to acquire knowledge". Dr. Carson developed his capacity in life as a youth via reading books and other literary works.

Reading provides the one with innovative mind set for self development towards achieving success and greatness in life attested to by the society.

The Holy Bible is the Book of Life and reading same gives one a fulfilled life of accomplishments. The Holy Bile knew the importance of reading and went to state that; my people perish for lack of knowledge.

All great achievers on this planet earth have linked their successes to reading books including the Holy Bible. Reading empowers one's mind to gain insights and revelation knowledge which when activated energizes one to work towards self development, discoveries, accomplishments, successes etc.

Anybody who devotes time towards reading becomes an exceptional person in the society. Any book that must develop one must first empower the mind. What we read is a replica of what we achieve in life which is a pointer towards self development.

Success and accomplishments of life are constructed and conceived in the heart- the mind through what we read. No wonder Napoleon Hill said "What the mind can conceive that it can achieve". Others who have also understood the power of reading after deep reflection includes Abraham Lincoln; former President of United States of America who said "The things I want to know are in the books… thus my best friend is the man who will give me books I have not read".

Reading leading to self development supports positive civic engagement of people, self reliance and entrepreneurship accomplishments, thus providing developmental values at all levels including communities. These activities that transform the society positively includes in the areas of political (governance, policy mobilization etc) and non-political (like community assignments, employment creation, talent discoveries etc), for which self development plays important roles in forming new life skills including leadership skills which drives positive change in the society.

Read. Read books. That is how to get someplace in life". (Kurt Schmoke, a lawyer and former Mayor of Baltimore, his message to young people). This is true for all persons who would want to develop himself and make meaningful contributions in the society.

In any self development efforts, the quality of the books we read also empowers our mind to start the process of thinking to live right and excel in life; through proper articulation of strong values; this is also true amongst the youths. If the youths embrace self development values, the students/ youths would do away with cultism, armed robbery, kidnapping and other social vices. They would rather engage themselves in entrepreneurship activities which lead to wealth creation, increase in productivity and value growth amongst the youths. Therefore, youth participation through self development in any nation contributes greatly to the growth of her national economy.

The world reckons with achievers. Failures have no role on this planet earth. Thus from creation God charged us to go into the world and take dominium. As we develop our minds via reading, we should strive to carve a niche in a particular area as to develop our personality and influence or dominate the society positively; the process of this is the process of self development; for which reading is highly instrumental.

Many people have attested to the fact that it was through reading that their lives changed and their contributions to societal development attested to.

Ogbo Awoke Ogbo, a Nigerian and founder of Giant thoughts International said "My father's library stirred me up to what I am today. I wish parents can inculcate reading in their children because it can transform their destinies for the better". He added, my father had this book titled, "Makers of Civilization", He said the book opened his eyes to what people could achieve in life. The leadership he provides today came as a result of reading.

In addition, Dr. Ben Carson a world acclaimed Neurologist and an international role model for many youths admitted that his success story became possible largely because he was encouraged to read books and also visited local libraries in order to learn and develop his mind which shaped his contributions to the society.

I, James Okere is also one person who have benefited from book reading and other literary works. The first book that gave me new line of positive thought in life is Napoleon Hill's book-"Think and Grow Rich". That book gave me new way of seeing things including developing the passion to read similar books leading to my being in a position to discuss on issues of self developing values.

Reading changes lives of people positively. The more we read, the more knowledge we get, improve our lives and the society we live in. The founder of Centre for Research Information Management and Media Development (CRIMMD) based in Nigeria; Dr. Raphael James says "We encourage people to read not because they want to sit for exams or go for an interview; read because you want to gain knowledge".

An empowered person through reading develops the society in diverse ways including meaningful socio-economic activities.

The ability to read wide especially quality books will go a long way to develop and fortify the mind of a person towards contributing to societal growth; a self development task.

In addition, developing reading culture amongst the youths would lead to youth's mentorship, inculcates leadership and management principles; which are core values of self and human development.

Reading gives us insights on various issues, thus helping one generate ideas on various issues as well. Most great people who have achieved great successes attested to by the people and society are men who developed time towards reading great books and other quality materials including books on successful men.

Finally, reading will lead one towards re-inventing his future; which would serve as a better future for all. Readers are Leaders is a popular saying that should galvanize us to embrace reading books towards self development leading to personal and societal development.

CHAPTER FOUR

TALENTS DEVELOPMENT

Dr. Myles Munroe a well known pastor, author and public speaker said ***"Anyone who develops his gifts will become a community".***

Talent is a sure way of self development in life. Talents are one's potentials deposited within a person. Talents are brain power for life accomplishments. They are gift from God. They are potentials that need to be identified by one. One need to think deep to become aware of these potentials endowed in him/her. In some cases through divine power one discovers these talents deposited in him or her. In some others, a person is aided to discover the potentials deposited in him via mentorship. Talents are built around one's vision of life.

Speaking on talents as it relates to self development, a Nigerian entrepreneur; Hakeem Belo-Osagie said ***"I think that one thing that makes you happy and successful is to know that your operating at the peak of your abilities".*** Talents vary from one individual and another. Some people could have talents in leadership, sports, writing, administration, analysis, acting, understanding, speaking, business etc. In the Holy Bible, talents are given special recognition or reckoning in that some people were discovered as Pastors, Evangelist, Prophets, and Apostles.

The Holy Bible recognized the role of talents in management of resources which was illustrated with the parable of talents (Mathew 25: 14-29). Also in the Holy Bible, the books of Romans 12: 6-8 and 1st Corinthians 12:27-30, recognized and listed various talents associated with us.

In addition, from Biblical accounts; Joseph had talent for dream interpretation, which eventually sky rocketed him to become a Prime Minister In a foreign land. Daniel also had gift for dream interpretation and excellent (leadership) spirit which gave him prominence when Nebuchadnezzar and Darius were kings in Babylonia. Jephthah had the talent of war management and execution which granted him success and recognition before the people of Israel.

History has records of people who have risen to greatness through their talents development and discovery. Kanu Nwankwo and Jay Jay Okocha developed their talent in football. Also Precious Uzoaru Dede; former Nigeria's senior female team no. 1 goal keeper and captain defiled opposition from his father to develop her talent. While Tiger Woods the world acclaimed golfer worked hard to develop his golf talent.

In addition, Chimanmanda Ngozi Adichie; a Nigerian has achieved greatness via her writing gift development. Dr. Ben Carson a world known neurosurgeon and role model for the world youths also worked hard to develop his writing talent leading to his publishing world famous inspiring and motivational books- "Gifted Hands" and "Think Big".

As noted above, gift or talents varies and are highly differentiated. In most cases, accomplished vision leading to great successes in life is as a result of talent discovery and development. When one's drives are geared towards his talents, then the person is bound to achieve great leap in life, even if it takes longer period. Countries and Nations that have discovered the need to develop the potentials of their citizenry have gone far in societal advancement.

Many great men and women who have changed the course of history in their countries in particular and the world at large are people that have identified their talents, persevered and developed same accordingly for the betterment of mankind and society. One thing that is remarkable with talent discovery is that it gives great recognition, which could take years in some cases. From such recognitions, further accomplishments and great exploits follows. These exploits arising from talent discovery are highly remunerated at the appropriate time.

We therefore need to create all the necessary awareness and enablement amongst the people (students/youths, men and women) to strive to develop their talents which would go a long way to improve the lives of the people now and in future. No matter the age of one, a person can re-write his history through looking inwards to rediscover and develop his talent. In this regard Dr. Myles Munroe said **"If you believe you're too old to use your gift, you're believing a lie".** It was at the age of 45 (forty five) years that Zig Zigla's talents in public speaking events manifested. Today, Ziglar accomplishments are known in the word.

One remarkable thing about talent is that it must be discovered and developed. If not discovered and developed, the talent lies within and the carrier stays without making any personal contribution, thus loosing societal recognition.

Nelson Ikechukwu Nwamara (a former mass communication student of Federal Polytechnic Oko, Anambra State, Eastern Nigeria) had the gift of writing and was further influenced by the works of Mike Awoyinfa's column in Saturday Sun (Nigerian Newspaper): titled Press clips. From his writing gift, imbued with courage, Nelson ventured into publishing as a student and became the publisher and Editor-in-Chief of Zestar Magazine (an inspirational work that serves the Staff and Students of Federal Polytechnic Oko Anambra State, Eastern Nigeria). This accomplishment gave Nelson societal recognition.

Talent identified could only be developed through great passion, courage, perseverance and action. In developing our talents we must keep faith alive and work assiduously to achieve same. Individuals should therefore strive to develop their talents and in so doing one's capacity is enhanced towards societal development. We require positive character, self discipline and self reinventing in our efforts to develop our individual potentials.

Following their strive to develop themselves, when you mention Fanny Crosby, you remember her as one who have developed and written several religious songs (talent development). When you mention George Bernard Shaw, Fannie Hurst, Charles Dickens, Chinua Achebe, Wole Soyinka you remember them as men that have conquered the literary world.

John Mikel Obi (a Nigerian) is an international recognized soccer star. He started playing soccer at Pepsi Academy and had played severally for local clubs. John continued developing his soccer talents until he graduated at a higher level of playing severally for Nigeria's national team. He is also an international footballer who has been part of the success story of Chelsea club London in lifting trophies like UEFA Champions, the Europe Club, and the F.A Cup. John's talent discovery and development has lifted him from obscurity to greatness.

Therefore, let us work towards developing our personality through developing one's talents.

CHAPTER FIVE

LOOK BEYOND YOUR CHALLENGES.

The truth is that anybody who wants to develop himself must look beyond his challenges. ***"Hardship often prepares ordinary people for an extraordinary destiny".*** (C.S. Lewis). We live in a world of challenges, thus any mind that is determined faces challenges. Difficult situations are part of human existence, and such human challenges are surmountable for a person who is eager to develop himself. Challenges could come to one through fears, family, community and social groups. It could also come through health, economic crises, persecutions, hatred, jealousy etc. Difficult situation could also come through lack of mentorship, encouragement and poor work environment. Loosing of job is a threatening challenge as well.

The challenges we face eats deep into a person, especially when not controlled. When we face difficult situations the most important thing that confront us is the attitude we adapt to confront same. In every challenge we face, there are opportunities that exist. Sunny Ojeagbese; a Nigerian publisher and motivational writer stated that ***"Adversity goes hand in hand with opportunity that is one secret of success people don't know"***. Thus in adversity or challenge of life, we must think deep, develop creative mind set and be willing to make adjustments in life if we are to personally advance in life.

In business world, frustration exists for investors and the mangers, but history has records of them that have remained focused, persevered and eventually succeeded. What is more frustrating for Walt Disney, who was looking for Banks assistance up to 301 Bank without success, but he persevered, looked beyond his challenges and approached the 302 Bank which came to his rescue in developing Disney World which the world has been enjoying for several years.

Social entrepreneurs who have set a task to solve a particular social problem faces difficult period of their time when beginning, but in such situation, they looked beyond their predicaments, strived in their endavours and succeeded later.

Joyce Meyer Bible Teacher, Author, Conference Speaker has repeatedly stated that she faced sexual harassment from her father and above all, she was not deterred , but eventually moved on and today she is highly celebrated following her accomplishments.

Precious Uzoaru Dede a Nigerian female footballer and national goal keeper faced great opposition from the father while trying to develop her football career, but she remained undaunted and at the end she excelled and rose to become Nigerian number one goal keeper, who contributed to the growth of soccer in Nigeria.

When we are faced with challenges, we should be trying in any positive endavour as to come out of it. In such situation, we need to believe in God. We should see God as the source to come out of the situation. Believe in God will grant one the spiritual strength and guidance to move ahead of life.

In addition, in any difficult situation, we should believe in ourselves. Believing in ourselves includes thinking deep of the powers and this powers lies in us until put into use. Also to look beyond the challenges we face, we should develop our talents, gifts and abilities God endowed us with. Developing our talents have taken many people to greater level in life when faced with challenging cases.

Benjamin Franklin longed to write for his older brother's newspaper where he worked as a printing apprentice but his brother refusal to let him. Ben wrote stories anyway, under a pen name, Silence Dogood, a fictional widow who was very opionated, particularly on the issue of the treatment of women. Every letter was snuck under the printing shop's door at night to avoid discovery. After sixteen letters, Ben finally admitted that he was the writer and though he received quite a bit of positive attention from everyone else, his brother only grew angrier and more jealous. This resulted in Ben receiving beatings and finally running away. Ben never allowed his interest to die as a result of his brother's attitude.

Ben who looked beyond his challenges in the course of developing himself, eventually started his own printing shop and later owned a newspaper, the Pennsylvania Gazette, which under his supervision became the most successful in the colonies. Benjamin Franklin wrote a lot in influencing Americans that he became known as the America Man of Letters; who later knowing the importance of writing in life developed this motivating quote **"Writing is the beginning of all wealth"** Ben's commitment which also brought wonderful public image in his life, led him becoming a successful diplomat in American history.

In addition to the above, we must have the fighting spirit to champion a task that could excel us in life. Also, developing ideas that could change one's personality is also ideal. One could venture into writing, service rendering etc, we never knew where the universe could act upon to elevate a person.

Louis Armstrong, the Jazz artist, who reported applied to go to music school when he was a young man. At his audition, He was given scales to sing, but he could sing only the first two notes properly, and he was told he didn't have what it takes to be a musician. The story said that he cried at first because he had been rejected from the music programme, but he told his friends afterward, **"I know there's music in me, and they can't keep it out"**. He eventually became one of the most successful and beloved jazz musicians. He sold more records and made more money than scores of others who were more talented at singing. Now he is forever etched in the history of music, because he insisted in developing himself.

Louis Armstrong looked beyond his predicament, put his life into the gift he knew he had, and this gift made room for him.

Finally, to look beyond our challenges, we should persevere in an identified task. As we persevere, we continue in earnest to remain creative as to turn around the predicaments we found ourselves.

CHAPTER SIX

SUCCESS IN SELF DEVELOPMENT

Success comes through consistent development of one self. Thus if we persevere in developing our potentials we must surely succeed. In achieving success we pass through trials, rejections, delays and temptations.

Florence Chadwick developed herself and became a champion swimmer. In 1952, she attempted to swim a span of the peaceful Pacific Ocean between California's Catalina Island and the state coastline. As she began the twenty-six mile journey, she was accompanied by small boats of supporters who watched for sharks and were prepared to help Florence if she got hurt or grew tired. Thick fog rolled in after about fifteen hours of swimming.

Florence recalled that after already having spent so many hours navigating the waters with her body, she began to doubt her ability. She didn't think she could make it, but she kept going. She swam for another hour before asking to be pulled out, physically and emotionally exhausted. She was tired and in her mind the California coastline felt like it was a million miles away.

After she got into the boat, she learned she had stopped less than a mile short of her destination. Two months after Florence failed attempt, she tried again to swim from California coastline to Catalina Island. During the journey, the same thick fog set in, but this time she succeeded in reaching the shore. She came this far because she strived to develop her potentials.

Poly Emenike a Nigerian entrepreneur worked hard to develop himself. He stated that following the influence of Napoleon Hill's two books (Think and Grow Rich and Law of Success) which he read provided him ready ground and he therefore made several efforts to reach the Board members of Napoleon Hill Foundation. Poly Emenike's attempt to reach the board was difficult, but he remained consistent and persevered for ten years before he eventually reached the board.

This contact with the Board as a result of the influence of Napoleon Hill's book had tremendous influence on his business enterprise and brought him into lime light, when the board of Napoleon Hill Foundation decorated him with the Napoleon Hill Foundation Gold Medal Award and plaque in the year 2012. His effort in reading Napoleon's two books had tremendous influence in making him reach the board and being recorded in the history of the foundation as the only person outside United States of America to be honoured with such an award.

Poly Ike Emenike who found it difficult after the Nigerian civil war to pay his school fees, who took School Certificate Examination at the age of 32 years, is also today a holder of a doctorate degree, and in addition, he is the Chairman and Chief Executive Officer of NERO'S, a pharmaceutical company based in Nigeria, a feat he achieved through developing himself through reading.

James Okere is my humble self, when I took up the challenge in year 2013 in establishing my inspiring website www.inspireforgreatness.com towards becoming an inspirational writer. The dream I set for myself was to write and post one article once a week in my website. Taken off was easy for me until the first year was over in 2014. At a time, I was tide of continuing with my dream project, but I kept on encouraging and developing myself and thinking on the positive nature of the website which is geared towards empowering the people; men , women and youths with values of self and societal development. This dream has remained a sustainable factor in my inspirational blogging towards developing myself.

William Wilberforce as a Christian entered into the British Parliament at 21 years after a Cambridge education. Wilberforce developed love and concern for others and subsequently set his affection upon a cause that would affect the destinies of millions of people all over the world. He initiated and championed the formation of a law to abolish slave trade. For 46 years he fought this battle and won. The whole world was made a better place and the entire society and man was given a better code conduct as a result of his campaign and victory. What an impact life William Wilberforce lived through developing his life.

Dr. Oswald Smith developed himself and impacted the entire globe with evangelism; winning souls for Christ. His popular motto includes ***"The supreme task of the church is the evangelization of the world"***. He travelled wide to preach including Jamaica, New Zealand, Russia, Great Britain and many European countries. He won many souls and once it was said he fainted while preaching the gospel. Even suffering from attacks of malaria he preached the gospel as well. Dr. Oswald preached in more than sixty-six countries. Even with that outing he was quoted to have said "I am not satisfied". Today his accomplishments have challenged many in this respect; this came possible because he developed himself.

Ogbo Awoke Ogbo developed his reading capacity. He is a Nigerian and founder of Giant thoughts International identified the role of reading in his life and went further to state that;

> ***"My father's library stirred me up to what I am today. I wish parents can inculcate reading in their children because it can transform their destinies for the better".***

He added, my father had this book titled, "Makers of Civilization", there he read all the explorers, like Christopher Columbus, I read about the discovery of America etc. Ogbo who developed his reading ability at the age of eight, further stated that, what he read made him wonder as a young child how these people started all these as far back as the 15th century, what spurred them to dare and to start making efforts towards inventions and discoveries.

Chinedu Nsofor graduated from the University of Nigeria, Enugu State Eastern Nigeria. He is 27 years as at year 2017. Chinedu Nsofor set his vision of life and developed his goals to pursue as to impact life in his environment. While at the University he developed his dream project- WORK WHILE IN SCHOOL; a programme designed to encourage our undergraduate to start early to think on their future plan of life. As at present, he has secured partnership with the National Commission of Colleges of Education (in Nigeria). His idea has started creating impact in the Nigerian Society.

Success comes also through locating a mentor; this is what also raised James Owen to greater height in sports. Many years ago, James Owen wanted to become a great athlete in Europe. He sorts for the view of his coach; who gave him four keys to stardom: determination, dedication, discipline and attitude. James Owen started working on them. At the 1923 Berlin Olympics he got four gold medals and his record in long jump lasted for 25 years unbroken. He did not just have a goal, but he applied himself to the four vital keys for success.

Stephen Skinner a successful pharmacist had a dream to help other Christian entrepreneurs succeed greatly in life, and to do it, he developed a programme tagged "Life Message". Following his commitment spirit towards the programme, he launched a speaking, coaching and writing business. He committed himself and got his Life Message turned into a book titled "The 100 x Life: 7 Simple Daily Habits That will Transform Your Life, Unlock Your Greatest Potential, and Create a Life Beyond Your Wildest Dream". This his achievements were after he committed himself to attend a seminar programme titled- Amplify Workshop organized by Jonathan Miligan which took place in October 2015; and between October 2015 and December 2015 the book came out, and between December 2015 and April 2016 he also wrote and published 3 devotional books as supplements to his core book. His commitment improved highly his personality that created four income streams for him in book sales, speaking opportunities, coaching and online course.

The book sales alone created up to six ways in a month royalty, and in addition added to him speaking opportunities, coaching and online programmes. Within less than 12 months his commitment transformed his personality.

Developing ideas, and working towards realizing such dreams are sure way to achieve success in life.

CHAPTER SEVEN

THEY DARED AND DEVELOPED THEMSELVES

ZIG ZIGLAR.

A motivational author and speaker who was born into a rural agrarian family. Ziglar's father died, when he was just five years, living him and his siblings with the mother. To survive, the family was involved in periodical part-time jobs. Even at the age of four he was helping the family, and was also involved in milking cows before he was eight years.

He was eager to develop himself, thus Ziglar struggled with life until he had encounter with God who changed his world view and life. If not for God, Zig Ziglar would have been a frustrated person, and history would have no place for him. Today he is well recognized in USA and the world. To his credit he has authored many motivational books.

Ziglar's desire and dream to become a speaker was born in 1952, when he heard Bob Bale, a motivational speaker from Phoenix, Arizona U.S.A spoke at a seminar in Florence, South Carolina, U.S.A. Again to achieve his dream of being a motivational speaker was not easy at all. For sixteen years he struggled to get speaking engagements. However for his interest, the support of the family and his wife which encouraged him to continue in his quest. Ziglar admitted that the love of the wife and her prayers made the difference in his life, as he kept on believing God and also keeping a positive mental attitude to succeed.

On 4th July 1972 through, an interaction of an elderly African American woman who stayed in Ziglar's home, this woman talked about Jesus all the time, and Ziglar this time committed his life to Christ (though born into a Christian home and attended Church) and he became a new personality in Jesus. At the age of 45, Ziglar had a new beginning. His past attempts to succeed proved abortive, but all that changed when Christ came into his life.

His achievements grew that since 1972 he had not solicited a single engagement rather he had turned down engagements because his calendar was full. His business blossomed and grew highly. Ziglar established Ziglar's Training Systems based in Carrollton, Texas U.S.A where he is the Chairman and employs other persons working for him. The company is noted in offering sales, motivation and customer service training programmes to multiple companies and agencies. A wonderful feat he achieved because he dared, encouraged and developed himself.

FANNY CROSBY:

Fanny Crosby is one woman who developed herself and whose desire to succeed is second to none. She was blind and worked very hard to become a renowned song writer of our time. Fanny Crosby was born on 24th March, 1820 in New York, United States of America. At an early stage of her life (six weeks), she became blind through a sickness, and remained so till her death.

Through her grandmother, she was nurtured early in life with Christian virtues and the Holy Bible, which made it possible for Crosby to develop great affection for God, and the things of God as well. Such deep relationship with God, made it possible for her to develop high level of inspiration to write many songs that have shaped the lives and minds of many people.

Fanny never allowed her early life disability to hinder her striving to achieve greatness in life. With the drive to develop herself, she gained admission into an institution for the blind, where she received excellent education. She was in that institution for the blind for about 23 years, as a student, and later as a teacher. Later in life, Crosby got married to Mr. Alexander Van Alystne (a blind man a lover of music). Their union was blessed with a child who died in infancy. Crosby lived with her blind husband for 44 years before he died in 1902.

Fanny Crosby a highly determined person never allowed her predicament to deter her quest to develop herself, but rather remained resolute, and with utmost faith in God, she forged ahead for success. It is on record that through her industry, she wrote and produced about 200 songs each year. It is also on record that in her life time. She wrote more than 8,000 religious poems. Songs like **"Pass *Me Not Oh Gentle Saviour", "Blessed Assurance", "Rescue The Perishing"*** etc are her songs production. Crosby demonstrated that opportunities and successes are abound in any adversity for heart willing to develop herself, thus as a young girl in the Methodist Church in New York, she could repeat from memory the first five books of the Bible as well as many of the Psalms, Proverbs, Ruth, Songs of Solomon etc.

Following her successes painstakingly achieved, Crosby at a time was invited by the United States of America congress to recite her poems, which further proved her recognition and influence in the society.
Therefore, Fanny Crosby who saw many difficulties in her early life, however trusted God not to give up on life challenges, but remained resolute to surmount such obstacles that today she is reckoned for her successes in our society. She died on February 11, 1915 at a fulfilled age of 95 years. Fanny Crosby was indeed an epitome of a woman who developed her personality.

REUBEN MARTINEZ:

Reuben Martnez from Miami Arizona United States of America is one man who dared to develop himself. He demonstrated great vision and courage towards promoting reading and literacy values in the world.

Reuben's parents who were Mexican immigrants who worked in mines had no business in reading books. However, Reuben had vision towards reading. He admitted that his mother always wanted him to put down his book and clean the yard, but he insisted in developing his God given talent.

Following his interest in reading and literacy development, he went further to develop the required courage to continue, that even by 6.45 am every day, he would woke up and read his neighbor's newspapers brought by newspaper boy, thereafter, he folds back and kept the newspapers for the owner (his neighbour). His neighbour having seen Reuben's self will, went ahead to encourage Reuben. His vision also moved his teachers to assist him via lending him books. Reuben, later as opportunity came opened a barbershop, and continued with his visionary drive in literacy development leading to him using his barbershop to start lending the books he had collected to people to read; Reuben later stopped lending books as borrowers stopped returning the borrowed books, rather now selling books which he started with only two books, he sold in 1983.

His drive continued and he became an advocate for literacy via his life vision and courage demonstrated by him. Few years later, the barbershop with books became a book store; which he called **Libreria Martinez Books and Art Gallery** which has grown tremendously.

By his development drive and industry, as at year 2007, the store now store up to seventeen thousand titles and has become one of the country's largest collections of Spanish Language books. He has also opened more books stores.

For his vision and courage to promote literacy, he stated hosting a weekly cable show on Univision. He cofounded the Latino Book Festival with actor Edward James Olmos. Reuben stated speaking at Schools and to other groups to promote literacy. As his vision and courage in this area increases, in 2004, he won a MacArthur Foundation fellowship often called a **"genius grant"**- for fusing the roles of market place and community centre to inspire appreciation of literacy and literature and preserve Latino Literacy heritage.

In addition, for his self development, vision and courage, he received honourary doctorate in human letter from Whittier College in 2005, and was also named one of Inc.com's twenty-six most fascinating entrepreneurs.

Reuben Martinez vision and courage in life became tremendous leading to his achieving remarkable successes in global literacy development to prove that one's dream is achievable through vision and demonstrable courage.

TYLER PERRY:

Tyler Perry (famed playwright, director, actor and producer). To make it to Hollywood filmmaking was difficult, if not for his interest to develop himself. It would have led him to give up but he continued, and being a black worsened his case to realize his destiny in the area of film producing. Tyler Perry was from New Orleans's Seventh Ward. He fought a battle, developed a heart of an achiever and he succeeded.

At the age of twenty-two, Tyler wrote, directed and produced many stage plays that were financed with his personal savings. For more performances than he could count, only a handful of people showed up. This went on for years, but he persevered. He continued to save and invest his own money to produce the plays, but nothing seemed to take off and he remained patient with his destiny. Even when the cast performed to nearly empty house, Tyler never let go of his dream. He powered his dream and battled all obstacles to produce another play, even when no one had come to the previous one.

Tyler was even ridiculed by the Hollywood executives who told him, they could not back his movie because **"Black people don't go to the movies"**. He held on and refused to let go of his dream to write, direct, produce plays and movies.

Tyler was only fighting to keep his destiny, he wasn't fighting side battles of rejection, ridiculing etc. He invested his Warrior Spirit in fights that were worth the effort to get his plays and films produced. At a time he was homeless and slept in his automobile all in a bid to keep his dream alive. Because he never gave up, the winds of fate changed in his favour and he has since sold millions of theater and movies tickets to fans of his beloved Madea persona.

Tyler Perry made his brain work in the words of Kenyon E.W (author) who said ***"Make your brain work, it will sweat, but make it work, then it will improve, it will develop, until you become the envy of those around you"***. He worked to develop himself, remained tenacious towards his vision and he succeeded in his chosen profession.

PASTOR VINCENT N. PAUL:

Pastor Vincent Paul is an author of Persistence Works, a Captain (Military Chaplain) in the United States Army and President of Vincent Paul Ministries International. He gave his life to Christ at the age of 13 years in August 1985, and later answered the call into God's ministry.

Today through developing himself, he has published six books in his books on Persistence Book Series and has finished working on 10 others in the Persistence Series Books. He is at present a multi-gifted, motivational and notable preacher, teacher, healing evangelist, military Chaplain, prolific author and publisher.

Dr. Vincent also publishes persistence work in E- newsletter sent out weekly to several thousands of people in over 150 nations. He is the author of the book- **"Don't Be Discouraged"** (in this book he cited over 40 people who persisted and succeeded in life Vincent acknowledged that God inspires him to write and he writes by the grace of God

The above proves that God is the source of one's greatness. Your achieving greatness or walking into Greatness takes place here on planet earth. The earth is a creation of God. Your personality is a creation of God. Thus the first principle toward developing one's self and personality is walking in line with God's power.

> ***"When I was undergoing my undergraduate studies, I never knew I would become a writer. I grew up to discover that I was into writing. I grew p to discover that I was into writing ministry. The more I write, the more the gifts flourish".***

CHAPTER EIGHT

50 NUGGETS OF SELF DEVELOPMENT

ABRAHAM, Lincoln (Past U.S.A. President)
What you are, be a good one.

ALBERT, Dunnings
Great opportunities come to all, but many do not know that they have met them. The only preparation to take advantage of them is... to watch what each day brings.

ALBERT, Einstein (Renowned German Prof. of Physics)
In the middle of difficulty lie opportunities.

ANN, Giminez
Between you and anything significant will be giants in your path.

APPINS, Claudins
Every man is the architect of his own fortune.

ALEXANDER, Hamilton; a founding father of the USA and 1st Secretary of the Treasurer.

"Men give credit for genius; but all the genius I have lies in this: When I have a subject on hand I study it profoundly".

AUTHOR, Asher; a Tennis Champion
"One important key to success is self-confidence. An important key to self-confidence is preparation'.

BAN KI, Moon; Secretary General of the United Nations
"You may have to move obstacle on your journey to success, but when you arrive you will be much stronger for the effort'.

BEN, Carson; Medical Doctor, Author, Conference Speaker

"If you recognize your talents, use them appropriately, and choose a field that uses those talents, you will rise to the top of your field".

BENJAMIN, Disreali (British Statesman and Ex-Prime Minister)
"Imagination rules the world".

BENJAMIN, Franklyn (American Man of Letters)
It is observed that God has often called men to place of dignity and honour, when they have been busy in the honest employment of their vocation. Idleness is the Dead Sea that swallows all virtues, be active in business.

BETTE, Davis
Attempt the impossible in order to improve your work.

BERTRAND, Russell
Nothing is so exhausting as indecision.

BOB, Dr. Jones
It is better to die for something than to live for nothing.

BRIAN, Tracy; Author, Conference Speaker
When you develop yourself to the point where your belief in yourself is so strong that you know that you can accomplish almost anything you really want, your future will be unlimited".

BRUCE, Barton
"Nothing splendid has ever been achieved except by those who dared believe that something inside of them was superior to circumstances".

CHARLES, Dodgson
If you limit your actions in life to things that nobody could possibly find fault with, you will not do much.

CHARLES, Dr. Garfield
Peak performers are people who are committed to a compelling mission. It is very clear that they are deeply about what they do and their efforts.

CHARLES E. Wilson
The thing that contributes to anyone reaching the goal he wants is simply wanting that goal badly enough.
CHARLES, Kettering
Keep on going, and the chances are you will stumble on something perhaps when you are least expecting it.
CHARLES, Schwab; an Industrialist
"When a man has put a limit on what he will do, he has put a limit on what he can do".
CHRIS E. Kwakpovwe Dr.; a Nigerian Bishop, Pharmacist, Author
"If you stop dreaming, you will stop living. Dream dreams bigger than your head can carry. If your dreams are not bigger than your brain, God is not involved and you may not need Him. Dream dreams that create fear in you when you reason about them because it shows they are bigger than you but not your God".
C. S. Lewis
"Hardships often prepare ordinary people for an extraordinary destiny"
DANIEL, Ally; Founder of The Ally Way International in Washington D.C
"Critics make you do it better, haters make you do it faster".
DAVID, Blunt
"If you continue to do what is right, what is wrong and who is wrong will eventually leave your life."
DOUGLAS, Mac Arthur (General)
"Preparedness is the success and victory".
DAVID, Thoreau
If one advances confidently in the directions of his dreams, and endeavours to live the life he has imagined, he will meet with a success unexpected in common hours.
DAVID, Jordan
Self confidence gives you inner power and it commands the respect of your fellowmen.

DAVID, Seabury
Try out your ideas by visualizing them in action.
DOUGLAS, Mac Arthur (General)
"Preparedness is the success and victory".
DENNIS, Wholey
Expecting the world to treat you fairly because you are a good person is a little like expecting a bull not to attack you because you are a vegetarian.
DORTHEA, Brand
All that is necessary to break the spell of inertia and frustration is this: act as if it were impossible to fall.
EDWARD, Kramer
"Every man, woman and child has infinite potential just waiting to be trapped".
ELBERT, Hubbard
"A little more persistence, a little more effort, and what seemed hopeless failure may turn to global success".
HELEN, Keller
"Optimism is the faith that leads to achievement. Nothing can be done without hope and confidence".
HENRY, Cloud; Author, Psychologist
"We all make mistake but the people who thrive from their mistakes are the successful ones"
HENRY, Ford; Founder Ford Motors
"Before everything else, getting ready is the secret of success".
JIM, Rohn
"If you really want to do something, you'll find a way. If you don't, you'll find an excuse".
JOHANN, Wolfang von Goethe;
"Magic is believing yourself, if you can do that, you can make anything happen"
JOHN, C. Maxwell: Pastor, Author, Conference Speaker
"People who take initiative and work hard may succeed, or they may fail. But anyone who doesn't take initiative is almost guaranteed to fail".
JOHN, F. Kennedy: former USA President;
"Effort and courage are not enough without purpose and direction"
JOYCE, Meyer; Author, Bible Teacher, Preacher, Conference Speaker;

"Yes you can have the very best God offers, but you will have to be determined to never give up until you have succeeded in every area of life".
MYLES, Dr. Munroe; Pastor, Conference Speaker, Author, Educator, Leadership Mentor and Consultant

"Believe the dream in your heart and never doubt your ability to achieve your goals".
NELSON, Mandela
"It always seems impossible until it's done"
NORMAN, Vincent Pearle
No matter how hard things seem to be or actually are, raise your sight and see possibilities always here.
ORISEN, Swett Marden; Founder of Success Magazine
"There can be no great courage where there is no confidence or assurance and half the battle is in the conviction that we can do what we undertake".
PAUL, Kearley; Human Resources Professional
"Confidence and people skills aren't developed just by measuring and planning everything, they grow through doing and learning from experience and by taking risks".
PRESTON, Vander Ven
"The only way any one can hope to achieve something is to first begin".
RALPH, Marston
"You've done it before and you can do it now. See the positive possibilities. Redirect the substantial energy of your frustration and turn it into positive, effective, unstoppable determination.

CHAPTER NINE

BE INSPIRED TO DEVELOP YOURSELF:

Dr. Myles Munroe in his book- Becoming a Leader said;. *Dr. Munroe further added that* ***"inspiration is the capacity to cause others to discover themselves, their purposes and their abilities, and to maximize their potential"***. This is the primary role of any inspiration action or activity. Mentorship, Talent Development, Reading Books etc are values one could key into, to become inspired and succeed in life.

Benjamin Franklyn: He was one of the Founding Fathers of the United States. Franklin was a renowned polymath and a leading author, printer, political theorist, politician, freemason, postmaster, scientist, inventor, and diplomat. Yet, we probably would not know his name if it was not his passion for reading. During his life, meat was very expensive to buy, so he became a vegetarian. He saved every penny he could to spend on all variety of books he could find to read. This made him the man the world remembers him today. **(Preaston VanderVen).**

Dr. Ben Carson a world known Neurologist stated **"There is just no limit to what people can accomplish when they develop their minds and use book to acquire knowledge"**. Dr. Carson developed his capacity in life as a youth via reading books and other literary works.

Ogbo Awoke Ogbo: a Nigerian and founder of Giant thoughts International said ***"My father's library stirred me up to what I am today. I wish parents can inculcate reading in their children because it can transform their destinies for the better"***. He added, my father had this book titled, "Makers of Civilization", which opened his eyes to what people could achieve in life.

James Okere; I read close to eighteen books in year-2016. This books I have read kept me going with my dream project- Inspiring the people to recreate their energy towards self accomplishments. In addition, these books I have read also helped in powering me further develop my writing skills via inspirational values columns and my website, www.inspireforgreatness.com Realizing the power of reading books, I now champion Reading Culture via Donate Book Project.

Talent development: When you mention Fanny Crosby, you remember her as one who have developed and written several religious songs (talent development). When you mention George Bernard Shaw, Fannie Hurst, Charles Dickens, Chinua

Achebe, Wole Soyinka you remember them as men that have conquered the literary world. Let us work towards developing our personality.

John Mikel Obi (a Nigerian) is an international recognized soccer star. He started playing soccer at Pepsi Academy and had played severally for local clubs. John continued developing his soccer talents until he graduated at a higher level of playing severally for Nigeria's national team. He is also an international footballer who has been part of the success story of Chelsea club London in lifting trophies like UEFA Champions, the Europe Club, and the F.A Cup. John's talent discovery and development has lifted him from obscurity to greatness.

Mentorship: Mrs. Funmi Adebayo, an engineer and lead consultant, Shophaholyks Solution dealing with ventures across the country (Nigeria), providing IT Solutions to businesses and organization speaking on the values the parents inculcated in her said;

> ***"They taught me about God. I grew up knowing God and I was never far from God because they taught me about God and about hard work. She added that the mummy taught her to be patient, to have good character and added that the mummy taught her not to talk when she was angry".***

On Seminar/Conference: To further develop one's capacity as to excel in life, we need to attend conferences/seminars which build our minds for life pursuits and greatness. Inspiring conferences have also become great way to influence one positively. The thoughts shared at such gathering shape one's mind sets towards accomplishments.

Pastor C. Maxwell; an internationally recognized leadership expert, speaker and author in his book the **21 Irrefutable Laws of Leadership** stated that several years ago while teaching leadership to a group of people in Denver U.S.A., he noticed the activities of **a nineteen year old named Brian**, who he said he spoke to and encouraged him thus "Brian, I've been watching you here", ***"I said, "and I'm impressed with how hungry you are to learn and glean and grow. I want to tell you a secret that will change your life".*** I believe that in about twenty years, you can be a great leader.

Pastor Maxwell further encouraged Brian to make himself a lifelong learner of leadership. Read books, listen to tapes regularly, and keep attending seminars. And whenever you come across a golden nugget of truth or a significant quote, file it away for the future. Today, Brian Tracy is an accomplished author, leadership expert and motivator.

Being inspire is a wakeup call challenging us to develop ourselves as to inculcate right values amongst the people; men, women and youths who are our future leaders. We have a duty to build one and another in this regard.

EPILOGUE:

Developing yourself has attempted to x-ray the values that propel one into accomplishments. Developing yourself involves personal initiatives and courage geared towards imbibing the culture of discovering oneself which includes going the extra mile in creating defined avenue for achieving greatness.

Imbibing negative values will not help us as individuals in our attempt to develop one's potentials in life. Negative values retard personal initiatives and the accompanying successes it would provide towards individual and societal development.

It is further identified that talent discovery and development has great influence towards self development. The few persons sited in this book were men and women who defiled their difficult environment to achieve excellence in life, through which society became transformed. The idea of complaining continuously about governmental policies or unfavourable conditions infinitely will not add value in assisting any person who would want to become a contributor for societal growth.

An identified way to come out of the world crises would be to firstly re-examine our thought process which should be tailored to galvanize our personal initiatives towards self-discovery and development as the few men and women discussed in this book did, in spite of the difficulties of their time. We can achieve same through faith, enthusiasm and determined mind.

Anybody who really wants to become a success story in life emulated by the people, such a person must strive to work on his gifts trust in God and himself.

Many people by their belief and lack of faith seem to have lost hope of personal initiatives towards advancing the cause of human society; we should change from this negative thought through developing one's potentials towards personal and societal development.

ABOUT THE AUTHOR

James Ngozi Okere studied Political Science at the University of Nigeria Nsukka, Eastern Nigeria and he is a member of Nigerian Institute of Management (MNIM),

He is also the author of the following books: A Rotary Hand Book For Rotaractors, 1995 Nigeria By The Year 2040 - Path To National Unity And Stability (A Nigerian Thought), 2001, Who Is Who (In Nigeria Fifty Years Of Political Quotes), 2002 and You Too Can Be Great (Core Value Self- Re- Orientation) 2011. James has many published works on Nigeria's political concepts. He enjoys reading, writing and thinking on developmental issues.

Presently, James Okere is an Author, a Social Entrepreneur and Project Coordinator of Inspire Foundation (IF) an NGO. Inspire Foundation (IF) is involved in educational issues covering self Enhancement and Advocacy in these areas: Mentorship, Entrepreneurship, Leadership, and Self Development values aimed at developing the people-men, women and students/youths for self realization and advancement for a better society.

His professional interest stretches from writing, inspirational blogger, public speaking, and strategic research to leadership development. He is active with community works and development.

In year 2013, Okere developed a website, www.inspireforgreatnesss.com the website promotes issues in leadership, mentorship, personality, entrepreneurship, inspirational nuggets, and governance.

Okere is a strong believer in prayers and holds that everybody is somebody. He lives in Owerri, Imo State Eastern Nigeria.

E-mail: info@inspireforgreatness.com , +2347035289205

www.ingramcontent.com/pod-product-compliance
Ingram Content Group UK Ltd.
Pitfield, Milton Keynes, MK11 3LW, UK
UKHW041905190726
13854UKWH00003B/1094